MW00720053

NATIVE CANADIANA

nAtive CANaDIANA

songs from the uRban rEz

GREGORY SCOFIELD

POLESTAR
BOOK PUBLISHERS

Native Canadiana / Songs From The Urban Rez

Copyright © 1996 by Gregory Scofield

No part of this publication may be reproduced, stored in a retrieval system or transmitted, in any form or by any means, without prior permission of the publisher or, in case of photocopying or other reprographic copying, a licence from CANCOPY (Canadian Copyright Licensing Agency), 6 Adelaide Street East, Suite 900, Toronto, Ontario, M5C 1H6.

The publisher would like to thank the Canada Council, the British Columbia Ministry of Small Business, Tourism and Culture, and the Department of Canadian Heritage for their ongoing financial assistance.

Mask created by Gregory Scofield
Cover photographs by Rosamond Norbury
Cover design by Jim Brennan
Editing by Patrick Lane
Printed and bound in Canada

POLESTAR BOOK PUBLISHERS
1011 Commercial Drive, Second Floor
Vancouver, British Columbia
Canada   V5L 3X1
(604) 251-9718

CANADIAN CATALOGUING IN PUBLICATION DATA
Scofield, Gregory A., 1966-
    Native Canadiana
ISBN 1-896095-12-7
        1. Indians of North America — Canada — Poetry. 2. Métis — Canada — Poetry. I. Title
PS8587.C614N37 1996   C811'54   C96-910007-8
PR9199.3.S297N37 1996

Hai-Hai Nitotemak

The author would like to gratefully acknowledge the Canada Council for its assistance in making this book possible; Patrick Lane for helping me sing the songs; love and thanks to Maria Campbell for her encouragement, guidance and support over the years; my wonderful publisher Michelle Benjamin at Polestar Book Publishers for believing in me; Julian Ross for his encouragement and guidance; Jim Wong Chu; Soloman Ratt at Saskatchewan Indian Federated College for the Cree spelling in *ni-âcimon*; my best friend and greatest fan Kelli Speirs; Carol Kellman, Annabel Webb & Kim Hiebert, for their neverending support, understanding and patient ear; Christopher Pinhey for his delicious humour and steady patience while I muddled through it all; sincere thanks and respect to my co-workers at Family Services; all my writer friends like Caroline Woodward, Joanne Arnott, Evan Adams, C.J. Taylor and many others who have shared their knowledge, support and talent; my many urban rez brothers and sisters who have so openly shared their pain, experiences and stories. And finally, I wish to acknowledge the many talented First Nations colleagues and colleagues of colour, be they writers, poets, actors or artists, who have given me the inspiration to sing my songs — to sing them the way my spirit remembers.

All My Relations
Greg Scofield / 1996

Some of these poems have appeared in their working form in *Breathing Fire: Canada's New Poets* (Harbour Publishing) and *Alphabet City*.

Native Canadiana / Songs From The Urban Rez

1 / Native Canadiana
The Poet Takes It Upon Himself To Speak / 11
ni-âcimon
>> 1966 / 16
>> 1972 / 18
>> 1975 / 20
>> 1981 / 22
>> 1985 / 24
>> 1986 / 27
>> 1993 / 30
>> 1996 / 31

Nikâwî / 32
Treats / 33
Lifetime Stranger / 35
Stepfather / 37
The Last Uncivilized Indian / 38
Kiddy Psych Ward / 40
Wrong Image / 42
She Was Dark / 45
Three Poems (legacy in the blood)
>> Blood Secret / 47
>> Blessing The Blood / 48
>> Blood and Tears / 49

ochichisa / 51
Policy of the Dispossessed / 53
Mixed Breed Act / 56
Not Too Polite Poetics / 59

2 / Songs
I Used To Be Sacred / 63
Âyahkwêw's Lodge / 66
Queenie / 68
Owls In The City / 71

Final Hours In The Lodge / 73
The One I Thought About Keeping / 75
Buck & Run / 78
Snake-dog / 81
The Trouble With Music / 82
ayamihâwina / 84
That Coyote Lover / 85
Promises / 86
For The Ones Who Got Away / 87
Who's Blue / 88
Going It Solo / 89
I Want / 91
Song For Dean / 93

3 / The Urban Rez

Tough Times On Moccasin Blvd / 97
Fix / 98
Day's Work / 100
tipiskâk / 102
Another Street Kid Just Died / 103
Shaky Ground / 104
Cycle / 106
Purple Moon Café / 109
How Many White People Noticed / 111
That Squawman Went Free / 113
No Fuss / 114
Leftovers / 115
Street Rite / 116
Piss 'n' Groan / 118
Warrior Mask / 121
The Poet Leaves A Parting Thought / 123

Cree Translations / 126

In the memory of *nîkawî*
my mother and friend
DOROTHY MAY SCOFIELD
April 1944 - January 1993

who sat with me
throughout the silent hours
forever encouraging

1

Native Canadiana

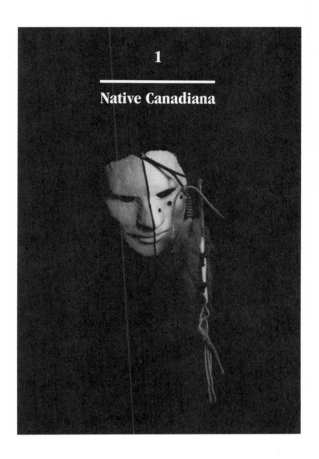

The Poet Takes It Upon Himself To Speak

1.

hâw-nikiskisin
first the language
was old earth,
clumps beneath the water
Wîsahkecâhk begged
Muskrat to bring up,
expanded into an island.

Maybe it happened like this:

our *ayamihâwina* floated
as far as Spain
needed purification, censoring
so hymns would stretch,
trail the wagon road
to church —

maybe
our ancient speakers
crammed wafers in mouthfulls
forgot their buffalo tongues
so our mouths hungered
stomped on grapes —

maybe the *pîkiskwewina*
got away from us
locked in the attic
so the only sound
was hooves clomping —

maybe
the sound was pleading
immaculate light
in the dark —

maybe
we talked in pillows,
in the school-yard, at Mass.
maybe
we conversed in secret
retaining
bits of earth, sky.

---

bâw-nikiskisin: now, I remember
Wîsahkecâhk: First Man or Cree Trickster
ayamihâwina: rituals
pîkiskwewina: words

2.

I always thought
it was the piss-moon,
the yellow ring
scalding my baby tongue
making conversation sour,
foreign.

In school
it was never discussed.
Columbus
may have tasted
salt-water spray.
He just discovered
the country, pissed anywhere
that was it.

At first
their English was trouble
but convinced
my lazy tongue
flopped involuntarily,
a whitefish
gasping fresh lake water.

Again I thought
that damn piss-moon
curse
tagging behind.

It was the same moon
glowing hot
from my aunty's mouth
while drinking.
Those demon fire-balls
bounced in my head
and became stories.
Mornings
I thought I heard them
rumbling her guts
behind the bathroom door.

Years later
I met others downtown,
all piss-moon talkers.
The yellow lines
dividing the road
said which side
we belonged on.
The alley or ditch
was where we pissed,
all swapping coyote scents,
charming
the scarred moon face
out of her
shameful silence.

3.

hâw-nikiskisin

the language was spoken,
always spoken.

êkwa êkosi kîtohta!

---

hâw-nikiskisin: now, I remember
êkwa êkosi kîtohta: and so, listen

ni-âcimon / Autobiography

osâm ôki piko mâmitonêyihchikâna kâkikê-kâ-pimâtisicik
Because only the memories live forever

1966

The *mâmitonêyihchikâna*
spilled from her mouth
and trickled
in spurts, me a dry bed
thirsting *âcimowina.*

La Ronge, Lynn Lake
were dots on a map
revisited by my finger.
The *pîpîsis* before me
floated around blue inside
and went silently with her
to the grave.

But *kîwetinohk*
I remember
Whitehorse
we lived in an old trailer
until the house was built.
The bush was our playground.
A team of huskies
pulled us kids around
kissing our snotty noses
where icicles hung.

kâ-miyoskamik
the pups got sold.
At five
I developed a tendency
to whimper, howl
inconsolably.

---

mâmitonêyihchikâna: memories
âcimowina: stories
pîpîsis: baby
kîwetinohk: the north
kâ-miyoskamik: springtime

1972

The *maskêkiyiniwak*
said the lupus
was all in her head.
The arthritis wasn't a lizard
crippling her bones
but severe depression.
So they shipped her off
to a psych ward in Edmonton
where they fixed her brain
by zapping it — seventy times
to be exact.

My school picture
stood by her bed, a stranger
she had to ask
who's this.
âskaw kâ-tipiskâk
she'd wake up crying
because she dreamt
the north country
and my laughter.

Six hundred miles south
I hid in a maple tree
thinking of Canada.
tahto kîsikâw
I waited for the phone to ring.

Three years
the leaves bloomed green,
turned brown and broke
into flight
until

one day

she came.

---

maskêkiyiniwak: doctors
âskaw kâ-tipiskâk: sometimes at night
tahto kîsikâw: every day

1975

êkospî kâ-nîpihk
it was just her and me
living at the Marlo Inn
on 224th Street —
Welfare River Town,
people called it.

She'd just gotten out of treatment
and strutted around
like no one's business.
A.A. meeting nights
I sailed the Love Boat
drove crazy with Baretta
ear poised
awaiting her flip-flops.

She met him
at one of those meetings.
All I knew
he was a reformed army boozer.
It didn't seem to matter.
In the dark
my mouth practiced
that word, dad.
Then one day
he came

and stayed.

♦

He had black *kinêpik* eyes
that slithered around
serpentine, always lurching.
êkospî kâ-kî-pîkiskwêt
it was rolling
thick clouds overhead.
He puffed his Export A
like a tough *nehiyaw*
and I caught
the back of his hand
for asking.

He was a Black Scot
Goddamn it
and proud
not some bloody Indian
who bumped around
glass-eyed upstairs.

That summer
I was nine
smelling of fear and hate.
In my pillow
I sang down his thundering fists,
her muffled cries, spitting
venomous
my dark curse.

êkospî kâ-nîpihk: that summer
kinêpik: snake
êkospî kâ-kî-pîkiskwêt: when he spoke
nehiyaw: Indian

1981

Damn Fuckin' straight
my talk
was hard pissed-on streets,
no pussy footing around.
My first place
was an attic suite
with a double burner stove.
Canned soup and vodka
it was

freedom.

I was the *sîpihko-nâpêsis*
with olive smooth skin
and lips
that pouted innuendo, tempting
as the canyon's edge.
nâpêwak
crammed around me
in leather bars, generous
as any piranha.
I was a skinned carcass
giving off
a sweet, succulent scent.

My first *nîcimos*
was twenty-seven
rubbed
my back   one night
grabbed
between my legs
the day after
I turned sixteen.
I shacked up thinking
all I had to do
was keep giggling.
At school
word got around
I was a contaminated fruit.

êkospî ê-miyoskamik
I overdosed
for the third time
unsuccessfully.

---

sîpihko-nâpêsis: Blue Boy (as in the painting)
nâpêwak: men
nîcimos: sweetheart or lover
êkospî ê-miyoskamik: that spring

1985

The Trans-Canada
was a green snake
winding
endless through my eyes
each mile shedding my neon skin.
In the north
the totems
whispered to the sky
and stared
sentry watching me walk
the one gravel road
connecting the reserve.

Autumn mornings
the medicine bear *ahcâhk*
lingered, poked around
inside
birthing her ceremony
preparing sacred
my winter dreaming den.
Nights
I dreamt my hair
a braided river cascading.
I was sober
one year, three months.

◆

êkospî ê-pipohk
Barb's brother
shot a black bear.
The first cut
I made
shaking and unsteady.
The carcass just laid
sprawled
on its back, eyeing me
shameful.
The glow of the flood lamp
was *Wîhtikôw*'s eye
laughing in the dark
while I hacked
each claw.
At a party
a beer was offered.

Six months
on their rez
I was told
if ever I married
someone would put a bullet
in my head.
My drunk talk
was a halfbreed brigade
armed and ready.
Their mouths
were a winchester
cocked and hidden.

In Saskatoon
I escaped to the lumpy bed
my *nitim*'s cousin provided.
Her old man
was in jail
so it was okay.
At the Albany Hotel
I learned
busted lips were from
not sitting stiff
with my back to the wall.
My first black-out
I was a tranquilized bear
dumped
somewhere between 20th Street
and the railroad tracks.

That bear claw necklace
hung about my bed
reminding me of my cannibal sins
until the day
I sold it.

---

ahcâhk: spirit
êkospî ê-pipohk: that winter
Wîhtikôw: cannibal or Ice Being
nitim: sister-in-law

1986

One lousy food voucher
held up the line,
my worker's generosity
was the half-empty bag
I lugged home.
Outside the music store
hot tears
drenched my Opry dream
and scorched
my throat permanently.
My first poem
was a stub pencil
scrawling notes
on brown paper.

At the community college
downtown
she was the brown face
I confided in.
She talked
distantly of being
slapped at the residential school
how
for years after
she wandered homeless
in her bones.

My twenty-first birthday
she took me for dinner
and planted
a garden in my heart.

The following Friday
she dropped by, told me
to pack some things.
"*kâya kakwêchihkêmaw,*" she said,
"*sôskwac itôta.*"
We drove north past Duck Lake
barely talking
then she simply whispered,
"Greg, *pekîwe.*"

In the middle of the prairie
I sat
tearing my *Cheechum*'s lodge
screeching
at 101 years of defeat
to the indigo sky
tasting
the salty blood
of buffalo, rabbit and gopher
that ran ancient
through my veins and
gave life
to our history, the fiddle
as it waltzed
through the empty coulees
at Batoche.

êkospî kâ-tipiskâk
the first seed
sprouted
then another and another
until my flesh, my bones
were as rooted
as the sweetgrass
swaying
as far as
the eye could see.

---

kâya kakwêchihkêmaw: don't ask
sôskwac itôta: just do it
pekîwe: come home
Cheechum: great grandmother
êkospî kâ-tipiskâk: that night

1993

I wheeled her downstairs
outside
she sat smoking, her
tiny feet tucked
under the hospital blanket.
The first manuscript
she clutched,
a proud tear
formed and spattered.
She'd heard
ni-âcimon
before me.
Every blackened eye, each smile
was the silent warrior
guiding my pen
across the page.
She was buried
in her starblanket
and cowboy boots.
I had the fiddlers play
"Whispering Hope"

---

nî-âcimôn: autobiography or My Story

1996

I am not ashamed
to admit
I still howl
inconsolably.
The stars too
will be my path
to grandmother moon.
In the dreaming hours
my stones I carry, and
cast
until the last
is shed, and
my feet know the sky.
kaskitêw-maskwa / nimâmâ
keeps watch.
My black bear / mother
keeps watch.

---

kaskitêw-maskwa / nimâmâ: my black bear / mother

Nikâwî

The world began
through the V of her legs,
a wishbone expanding
that never broke.

My right foot
lodged between her ribcage
was only a hint
of the pain to come.

Thirteen hours it took
before she could breathe
Paskowi-pîsim
into my mouth   and smile.

Twenty-nine summers
the Moulting Moon eclipsed
his ghost
never once disturbed my dreams
not even
when the phone rang and rang
that's how missed he was.

Paskowi-pîsim: July or the Moulting Moon

Treats

I can't remember exactly when
the taste started
only that it came
one night
she grabbed her coat,
told me to wait.

The last time
I hollered, made such a fuss
this time
I wound up tagging along.

Hand in hand
we set out,
down the hill
past the bootlegger's shack,
my hungry eyes
spying for the first time
lonesome alleys, phantom dogs
on midnight streets.

After dark, she said
always walk
in the middle of the road.
And never,
ever get into cars.

Outside the hotel
safely tucked
behind the dumpster
she told me
count to a hundred.
Don't go anywhere,
don't talk to anyone —
just wait.

81, 82, 83
my black bear mother
slight as deer, soft as rabbit
toting her six-pack
slipped into my hand
the salmon jerky treat.

Lifetime Stranger

Mostly I was a vacant-eyed kid
thinking of him
especially when she drank.
The three pictures I had
I hid in the top drawer,
his fat brown face
under my socks and t-shirts.

When I was older
I started to think
maybe he wasn't
who she said
he was.
I wanted wedding pictures,
divorce papers,
a birth certificate — an answer
how come he never called
or came around.
Probably dead
or in jail, she'd say
shrugging her shoulders.

Finally
when I reached adulthood
I stopped probing,
took her silence to be
a wound never healed.
Sorting through her stuff
after she died
there wasn't one trace.

Even now, I wish
I hadn't ripped those pictures
so hastily
back then.

Stepfather

He stole the sun,
spoke thunder
coming down the mountain
only too proud
to swallow the last rays.

Like raven
he kept any warmth
sealed tight
in a box.
Never ask or beg
she said, her eyes
loose hinges
on a swinging door.

I knew then
not all storms
were good.

The Last Uncivilized Indian

All throughout my teens
I tried hard
keeping out of sight,
keeping quiet, keeping
shut-up in my room
pillow over my head
to drown out
her screams.

I remember Indians
trucking into town
for Midnight Mass,
none of them
seeing me seeing them
in the back pew.

It happened one Christmas
up north
after my mom got punched
for mouthing-off.
I ran the four miles
knee-deep in snow
panting the ice-ache
my stepfather left.

Already Mass had begun
so I crept in,
took the farthest seat
and waited for the ache
to be lifted.

(more impossible than
Mary & Joseph finding shelter)

Still I prayed for the miracle:

One happy family,
my mom's laughter,
his heart attack, dog attack,
Indian attack,
attack of the liver, lungs,
colon, gallbladder —
even his conscience.

That year
another three feet dropped
while praying.
Jesus was asleep,
safe until next year.
The long walk home
I could have gladly frozen.
A truck pulled up,
asked did I want a ride.
No, I chattered
plunging northward.

Kiddy Psych Ward

At fourteen
I trusted men
the way a mouse
trusts a snake.
My dreams were phantoms
fluttering
bat's wings, mad cries
of my stepfather
lurching
from back alleys, dragging me
down dark streets
crushing bone, stealing breath.

The last OD
was a handful of valium
which landed me there
and her worker
who said
if I didn't go
she'd get cut off welfare.
Who could argue —
the shack we called home
housed her pill collection,
the bottles under my bed
to ward off demons.

The first month
I was an island
far beyond
locked doors, antiseptic rooms,
barred windows

calculating the space between
and how to ease,
push, squeeze
my spirit through.

Then it happened most unexpected.
The kiss was disguised wine,
flavoured mint, snatched
one night at bedtime
his nose trailing my spine,
begging my hands
between his legs;
that hungry snake
becoming our secret
at night, during the day
his eyes following me,
coaxing the right answers
for nurses, doctors,
my mom.

Three months of perfect silence
he crept into my dreams,
exorcised the phantoms, hushed
the cries, destroyed
the demon

and brought others
so I was an ancient shell
vacant and floating
the soundless waves
beyond the window.

Wrong Image

Yeah, their necks were stiff
from watching Indians downtown
who'd piss in the back alley
closing time.
From their cars
they were safe, those honkies.
We knew they were there
skulking around
like a weak species
trying to build themselves up.

In high school
Emma and me
were the only Indians.
We started hanging out together
formed the very first
least likely to succeed club.
None of those white kids
could down a mickey
of rye like us.
We didn't even need a mixer —
just pop off the cap
and chug-a-lug.

Sometimes they'd stand
out on the street
straining to hear our drunk talk.
We spoked pretty broken
so when dey mimicked our dalk
it was authentic not Hollywood.

They joked about our appearance
said we picked
left-overs at Sally Ann.
Once at recess
we overheard them laughing
and gave each one
a damn good wallop.

In the school library
where I thought and brooded
a long time
I crouched over history books
staring sullen
at those stoical faces.
Me and Emma
got names too.
I was her chief
and she my squaw —
only she humped anything
I was too stupid to notice.

Last summer
I spent the afternoon with a journalist.
I wore linen and leather sandals,
spoke of racism and class
and why I began writing.
The interview was about survival
and healing.
In the article
I read he was disturbed

by the predominance of alcohol
in my work —
how I perpetuated
the negative image of native people.

Walking the beach later
so many white skins
sprawled and craving
earth colouring, a cool beer
I smiled stupid and wondered
whatever became of Emma.

She Was Dark

We only knew her
as Grandma.
Her *pahkwêsikan*
was thick and fluffy,
never flat or chewy.
She used milk and eggs
so we called it proper,
tea-biscuits.

The *wiyâs*
was always Grade A.
Her *la-patakwa*
were either baked or mashed,
never fire-roasted.
Dessert was vanilla pudding or cake,
never chocolate.

The sheets
were white and boarding school starched,
always tucked just so.
Her *âcimôwina*
was Cinderella or Red Riding Hood,
never *Wîsahkecâhk* or *Wîhtikôw*.
I didn't think to ask.

Years later
in her kitchen
I recited the Three Bears
nîsto-maskwak, in Cree.
"Mm-huh," she said
examining her dark hands
without looking.

---

pahkwêsikan: bannock
wiyâs: meat
la-pataka: potatoes
âcimôwina: stories
Wîsahkecâhk: First Man or Cree Trickster
Wîtikôw: Ice Being or cannibal
nîsto-maskwak: Three Bears

Three Poems (legacy in the blood)

Blood Secret

She was someone else's
dirty *Cheechum* story.
The manager probably said,
get that drunk squaw outta here
when they finally found her
stretched out cold
on the floor, by the bed
wearing her fox coat & boots
ready to go.

Years later
it was my grandmother who asked
how she died.
A broken heart, my *mosôm* said,
dismissing the topic as if
it wasn't his to begin with.

Cheechum: great grandmother
mosôm: grandfather

Blessing The Blood

He was a good man —
he died too early,
my mom would say
when I asked
something about our history.
At school,
ethnic day I dressed
in a tartan kilt.
My face had
brown pigment marks.
I was convinced
God had yet to decide
what colour I'd be
so I stopped asking
and waited
for the significant change.

She listened to Wilf Carter
and Kitty Wells
sipping dainty her Old Style.
One time
I came home from school
crying because this kid said,
fuckin' welfare chug.
Never mind, she said
at bedtime,
you're my special blessing.

Blood and Tears

When the doctors
called a meeting
and needed my signature
it was final.
She just laid there
blinking silent tears,
the respirator pumping
phony life into her body.
I spent an endless month
singing all the old songs.
My voice never wavered,
cracked or choked
once.

January 12, 1993 — 6:38 a.m.
only then did I cry,
scream, rush about the room
like a trapped bird
looking to grasp
any piece of my history.

Now
nothing remains
but old warped records,
pictures, bits of memorabilia
and lost relations scattered.
In the other world
a fiddler arches his bow.

What remains
in the blood
is the Red River coursing —
and is spoken here.

ochichisa / her hands

they were the same hands
that changed diapers /
gave whippings /
held and spoke volumes /
all throughout
the turbulent years /
and finally
the silent hours /
when I pleaded
for even a disjointed memory /
something tangible
to hold onto like green /
her favourite colour
even the sickly green
of soiled bedsheets
or curtains
that wisp shut
in one motion /
I could tolerate / even stand
if it weren't for her
pushing mine away
or squeezing them
with the knowledge
of her leaving /
that I refused to accept
because they were
still so strong
from my hanging on /
and the diligent vigil
I kept / praying
for the lush green

of spring / or an end
to the orphaned winter /
until there was nothing
to pray for / hope for /
hold onto / for the last time
I held those same hands
that changed diapers /
gave whippings /
held and spoke volumes /
all in such a short
short time

Policy of the Dispossessed

And whereas, it is expedient, towards the extinguishment of the Indian Title to lands in the Province, to appropriate a portion of such ungranted lands, to the extent of one million four hundred thousand acres thereof, for the benefit of the families of the halfbreed residents.
Manitoba Act of 1870 — Section 31

That phrase (the extinguishment of the Indian Title) was an incorrect one, because the halfbreed did not allow themselves to be Indians. If they are Indians, they go with the tribe; if they are halfbreeds they are whites, and they stand in exactly the same relation to the Hudson Bay Company and Canada as if they were altogether white.
Sir John A. Macdonald,
Official Report of the Debates of the
House of Commons, July 6, 1885

In that part of the country
our homeland
they ended up squatting
anywhere there was road allowance.
My great-great grandmother's people
refused to be pushed out —
even after the first Resistance in 1869.
They lived in a vacant CPR shack,
watched the influx of newcomers
until one day
the prairie was completely taken over.

In that part of the country
our motherland
they gathered seneca root
or did odd jobs for white farmers.
When the jobs grew scarce

or ran out altogether
they perfected their English —
wiped away any trace of a dark language.
This I am told
was the death of *our nation*
and the birth of Confederacy.

In that part of the country
all public lands
were sold or snatched up by speculators
or shifty dealers in Métis scrip.
There are some deceptions left unmentioned.
The children's scrip, for example, in which
land was granted and sweet-talked
for chocolate bars or candies.
My *Cheechum* was born clutching prairie dust.
A taste of shame
clung on her rabbit / gopher tongue
and carried over fire generations.

In that part of the country
Canada
they hung around small towns,
outside the bar.
A bottle was planted in my *mosôm*'s hand
the day of his birth.
At thirteen he left that part of the country
and headed west to Saskatchewan and later
married my grandmother
who grew up on a farm, safe from any Indians.

In that part of the country
our homeland
I went back and dug in the prairie soil.
There among the buffalo bones and memories
an ancient language sprang from the earth
and wet my parched tongue.
In that part of the country
we were always *katipâmsôchik* —
and our displaced history
is as solid as every railroad tie
pounded into place, linking
each stolen province.

Cheechum: great grandmother
mosôm: grandfather
katipâmsôchik: The People Who Own Themselves

Mixed Breed Act

How do I act   I act without an Indian act
Fact is I'm so exact about the facts
I act up when I get told I don't count
Because my act's not written

So I don't get told who I am or where to go
If I want to hang solo without my tribe
Check out other rezless Indians
No DIA director can pop me on a bus

Send me home   homeless as I am
I'm exact about my rights
So exact in fact I act downright radical
Though never hostile unless provoked

To extract the truth
Truth is my treaty number's not listed
So I don't get obscene phone calls
From politicians breathing heavy in my ear

Or dirty Bill C31 talk
Still I'm authentic enough to be counted
A genuine artifact not so much precolumbian
But darn close

So I mark my X for self-government
And wait to be noticed
Not me alone as extinct
But distinct as we are

Once we were good enough
To be aboriginal even original Canadians
Way back before they took up hockey
And claimed our lakes

Those immigrants were too busy
Playing hookey on our grandmothers
To notice they left behind a new nation
To run their stolen country

Colonized as it was
It was already occupied and never sold
Why defend our claim
Both sides end up taking all the credit

So we end up scrunched in between
Suffocating ourselves to act accordingly
However we're told to act
But according to their act

I'm not soley a First Nations act
Or Canadian act
But a mixed breed act
Acting out for equality

This is not some rebel halfbreed act
I just scribbled down for revenge
Besides
I don't need to be hung

For my mixed mouth blabbing
How they used their act
To cover up
Dirty goings-on in our country

Not Too Polite Poetics

his diagnosis was not conclusively cutting edge
nor was the conversation charming
like was a I closet peace pipe smoker
or did I eat rabbits
with the fur still on

but what was my tee-pee creeping technique
did I make my move closing time
sneak up cruise past
make those heads tilt eyes swing
just this way, boy

or simply hang around
looking seductively stoic
like a Curtis portrait
waiting and contemplating
their move

out west I discovered
I didn't need to kiss up
to graduate head of the class
despite the prerequisite
keeping my mouth in check

not polite to stick my grudge nose
in their Native Lit class
say my piece on First Nations first voice
demand Kinsella visit Hobbema
or take a course in Cree colloquial syntax

like all First Nations writers
I must adhere to ethnic demands
make my poet's entrance
wrapped in a Pendelton blanket
sunburst geometric design

maybe a Navajo ring or two
to give me the authentic look
a ghost dance shirt
might come in handy
reflecting history bullets

when I get too mouthy
for their comfort
they want Yeats Dickinson Longfellow
a cosy chit-chat afterward

I barely pass the visiting poet's test,
answer why I'm so angry
so impolite, so defensive
is not what I want here
but the chance to speak

without backs up or a drum solo

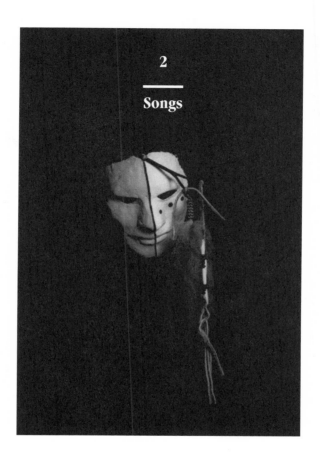

2

Songs

I Used To Be Sacred (on Turtle Island)

The first Two-Spirit didn't come about
because the Great Mystery was having
a confused day.
We got put on Turtle Island
for a reason — that wasn't
just to hang around the city
looking desperate
for other outcasts or acceptance.
I wasn't created
to be a lonesome turtle
crawling around by myself
(though none of these turtles
are worth beach-combing)
or duck under my shell
when someone takes a mean poke.

Just yesterday I was nosing around
at a turtle's pace
thinking
what an urban turtle like me
should do
when some big tortoise
nudged up alongside,
wanted to know
where all the best turtles go.
By his nose
I could tell
he wasn't from around here.

At first
I was flattered, tilted
my head slowly
and gave a turtle grin.
Then I saw
the red stripe on his neck
so I just shrugged, said
I didn't know.

Sure enough
three blocks later
that pushy bugger
still trailing me
wanted coffee, directions
to my nest.
Look, I snapped
I gotta big mean tortoise daddy
at home.

Pissed off, he tottered along
snorting his hooked nose.
So much for brotherly turtleship
I thought
that one would make good soup
at a Two-Spirited gathering.

Despite these beefy walruses,
cruisy sea-lions
and trendy urchins
I'm still for the most part sacred.
I even know
turquoise is a protection stone,
mined from the belly
of Mother Earth.

From month to month
I just plug along
watching my shell
doesn't get too chipped or cracked.
Often my moontime isn't regular —
though I'm a regular bleeding heart.
So what if I get too bloated
with words or opinions.
Why have to ask
who's who
and what's their story
on Turtle Island.

Âyahkwêw's Lodge

for Garry G.

êkwa êkosi, nikîwêhtatânân ôhi mistatimwak
and gave them to our women
who in turn
gave them to our men.
That night a baby was born in camp,
eyes clenched shut,
first in his mouth.

In the lodge
there was an old woman
who had woken in the night
to a lightless presence.
She was instructed
to make offerings,
bring water and blood
from the sacred woman's belly.

These she took to *Âyahkwêw*.

In the blood
a twinning spirit was seen.
The water
was marked by thunder.
Âyahkwêw prepared the rattle,
placing inside
the child's umbilical cord.

At dawn, the time of prayer
they brought the child
to our lodge to be named —
and so we named him twice,
Mistatim-awâsis /
He Who Calls *Piyesîwak-iskwêw*.

êkwa êkosi, nikîwêhtatânân ôhi mistatimwak: And so, we brought
    these horses home
Âyahkwêw: loosely translated as a person who has both male and female
    spirits; also known as Two-Spirited
Mistatim-awâsis: Horse-child
Piyesîwak-iskwêw: Thunder-woman

Queenie

When first
I heard Queenie was sick
I went out of my head
thinking
I too would be a goner
in couple of years,
maybe months, even days.

Death came to me
on a bus traveling west
back to the city
from where I was born.
I thought for sure
it would be the last time
I saw the world
with clear, undarkened eyes.

Already the funeral was planned;

I would be wrapped
in a starblanket,
my smudge feather
held between icy hands,
the red woven sash
binding my bony hips —
and the fiddlers playing
my spirit up & beyond
the Milky Way.

Queenie wanted to be
six feet deep before thirty
and got his wish,
though he gained
seven extra years
(probably the booze
preserving his insides)
Around the city
he got that name
from other Two-Spirits
who grew up on the same rez.

It was his mother's name
because she was bossy.
He was just like her, Queenie,
always telling you
what to do.

The carved silver ring
he gave me at sixteen
with his clan design
was like a wedding ring.
All throughout my teens
I kept it stashed away
for safe keeping.
Finally
I pawned it when I went straight —
although I tell people

I lost it somewhere
between Vancouver and Saskatchewan.

Somehow
they didn't need to know
until now.

In another life
I sure loved him.

Owls In The City

for my Âyahkwêw *relations*

The ones I remember
like Donny, Ray,
Felicia and Queenie
are all sick or dead
or just about.
They were the coyote ones
slumped together
at the Dufferin
eyeing every white guy
who walked by.
Back then
I was the chicken
of the bunch and
mouthy as any redneck.
Because I screamed and hollered
they kept out of my pants.

It was the ones
from back home
I had to watch.
Given half a chance
they'd tear into you
like a badger, fly off the handle
if you pissed them off.
Being a kid
I was hardly a contender.
I just stayed clear of them,
observed their *mâhkêsis* ways
from across the bar.

That was back in the '80s
before the plague really hit.
What did we know?
Everything about snagging was easy,
no one thought beyond the party.
Today it's worse —
our *iyiniwak* are dropping
like rotten chokecherries
in back alleys or hospitals.
Even owls have migrated to the city,
perched on rooftops or clotheslines
hooting their miserable death chant.

Tonight at the darkened window
tapping softly my drum, I think
how fortunate I am —
saved to pull up these *Âyahkwêw* songs
from my still beating heart.

Âyahkwêw: loosely translated as a person who has both male and female
    spirits; also known as Two-Spirited
mâkêsis: fox
iyiniwak: people

Final Hours In The Lodge (the rootbeer poem)

for Maui

From the bed
he sips the summer moon
without tasting
winter frost weaving
spider tracks across the window.
He looks past me, through me
waiting.

My mom wanted 7-up
my sister, orange crush
and him, rootbeer.
To see that kind of thirst
is to see how death
comes for each of us.

Is it our *nôhkomâk*
who light the fires inside,
sit hunched over
re-telling our *mamitonêyihchikâna*
until the lodge is cold
and finally empty?

From the 10th floor
I watch the city beetles
scurry below, rush nowhere
but everywhere important.
He watches me, mouth gaping
eyes black and smoky
as the fire-bitten coulees.

Each day I bring more rootbeer,
watch the inferno blaze,
wait   and so I will

until

the lodge is moonless and vacant
and I have only this memory,
among the others
to give to my grandmothers.

---

nôhkomâk: grandmothers
mamitonêyihchikâna: memories

The One I Thought About Keeping

for T.R.

Though all of them
I thought about keeping
he was the one
who offered candles, incense
spiraling gold light
in the dark

until

he marked the pages
a red felt pen
check
for the ones
he thought powerful, moving.

In the shower
a new scent
slid between his thighs
while I waited,
my grudge nose losing sense.

The best ones
had corners folded
reserved for critique, praise
his neat white bending
pulling my mouth homeward
desperate to taste
a red prairie sun.

Afterward
in my ears, his hands

kept the eagle-bone whistle
screeching
and so I ghost danced,
circled his dreams
keeping each foot
firmly rooted.

The good ones
weren't red suns, piss-moons
that flavoured conversation
over coffee.
The good ones were islands
handed over,
drunk men who beat
blackened mothers, men
blackened by black men
shamed by whitemen
too shameless for words.

Towards morning
the rain brought cleansing.

It was the words, his words
I thumbed the dictionary for
not the broken dialect
floating in my memory
that became good poems.

Flying home
a salty ocean
slid over my face

and became an island
unconquered.

Only once
he fucked the drunk,
dirty poet
sage breath and all
smelling me clean earth
fresh from the sweatlodge
without knowing
Kisê-manitow's gifts.

Kisê-manitow: The Creator or Great Mystery

Buck & Run

Whoever knows my big buck taste
Knows I follow their trail
Strictly for sport
To see
If what they say is true
You can't keep
A colonized buck down.
(though I've never had problems
keeping them up)

Conceited bucks are an entirely
Different breed altogether
Whenever I put
The Indigenous moves on them
I always keep to the lingo
They understand
Hey pretty buck,
Wanna come to my tee-pee
And lie on some soft fur?
(you'd be surprised
how many develop a fur allergy
after it's over)

Maybe my spear tip
Is too blunt for them.
Good thing it's not razor sharp
I might be tempted
To deflate their egos.

I once landed
A smooth bar buck talker
Who preferred *mâsawêwin* activity
In the dark under a duvet.
(on top with the lights on
when really bombed)

Needless to say
Two weeks later I hit the trail.
Imagine how I felt
Discovering a muskrat
In buck's clothing.
First I had a hostile impulse
Then sympathy.
(poor confused muskuck
didn't know which end was up)

Since then my P. Eye tendency
Is keeping ahead
Of their every step.
Why get bucked around
Unnecessarily?
I always double back /
Check the trail
For invader footprints.
Each time my nose
Picks up their *kîmôc* scent.
Why hang my head in defeat?

These bucks
Are too sl/easy for me.

When it comes to delicacies
I prefer
The real bannock & jam type.
Okay with me
If they leave a few crumbs,
I won't buck & run.

---

mâsawêwin: sexual
kîmôc: sneaky or sly

Snake-dog

iyee   dat one I tinks
between looks   big *skônak*
wants a whole friggin' army
jump into da sack, his hands
wants to rattle me aroun'
shakes me up a bit
for Pete sake   whats he tinks
I'm s'posed da crawl over
says hey,
you gots a great *kinêpik* smile
how 'bout slitherin' back
ta my pad
buts I'm no desperate dog
no siree
I wants flute music, horses
a darn good dose
of dat love medicine

---

iyee: exclamation of disgust or disdain
skônak: female dog; also, a sexually promiscuous person
kinêpik: snake

The Trouble With Music

It alway happens:

the permeated silence,
the moon shifting to honey
deceiving molasses gold
so the echo
is how each one sang,
how they strummed
a harp of fingers
over his body
plucking the hidden notes
so the flesh, the spirit
danced.

When the robins sang
he rose each time
ground the beans
so the coffee was fresh,
the waking sweet
so first the taste
was apples, pastries
lingering blueberry,
cherry kisses.

Some mornings
it went without fuss.
The taste was muskegs
or marshy places
revisited.

Those mornings
the notes became songs,
endless overtures
that slipped into crevices
and cracks that snaked
the bare walls,

the same walls
he climbed
dodging daylight, dreaming
the lost honey moons
that dripped molasses gold
straining to taste
one celestial chord.

ayamihâwina / Rituals

Their *wiyâs* I smash,
grind alongside my sister-wives,
crush chokecherries and whisper,
curse them fatal
under our breath, later press
our mouths healing against flesh
and listen to coyote tales
knowing
we are not the first or last.

Our *nôhkom*'s stone
we kiss
and feed them
the labour of our scheming
all the while
believing
our medicines potent.

---

wiyâs: meat
nôhkom: grandmother

That Coyote Lover

for L.C.

Watch dat sneaky bugger
When I dakes a break   sniffs aroun' restless
Nose picks up he-dog scent   *wâk-wâh*
dat one be a fine one   beefy one
Mmm … I likes 'em a bit chunky
dat way I dickl ̃ ̃ 'em 'n' dakes my time

No kidding bi

Today he say
So he be ch
Sneaking o
domorrow
tinking su
Sulking a   s

---

wâk-wâh: Oh my goodness
kîmoc: sneaky or sly
nîcimos: sweetheart or lover

Promises

not always did I have an aversion
to shiny objects, convenient arrangements

beneath the buffalo robe

snuggle into him   temporary
the famine his doeskin fingers snail
across my lips of strawberry pleasure

beneath the buffalo robe

spread my arms, my legs
I offer moose tongue and berries
generations he devours in seconds

beneath the buffalo robe

I don't get sweet-talked easy
his hands know what to do
in the dark / light of day

beneath the buffalo robe

promises he whispers   temporary
the taste his foreign tongue snakes
through ravines, over valleys

beneath the buffalo robe

each kiss
history
lolls on the tip of my tongue

For The Ones Who Got Away

Nights I plotted
the perfect revenge

how

I would sneak kisses
plant them behind ears,
bury them
in soft folds of flesh
where desire lingers

where

heat comes freely,
sparks the place where
oceans came crashing

once

Who's Blue (over the losing)

Certainly not me

I hated those Annie Lennox songs

and driving that back road
at some ungodly hour
the world so gone
I felt almost alive
like I could reach up
grab hold of the sequined sky
pull it down
and over us, and no one
would have blinked an eye.

Truthfully
I hated the spontaneous hunger

the dinners missed,
the movies half-seen,
the dates unkept,
the bed made, unmade
made again.

Certainly
I hated you most of all

more than fingers
leaving blue streaks
on rainy windows,
more than silence
that settles
and songs that mute
when least expected.

Going It Solo

It's not so much
I mind anymore, even care.
Given the choice
I'd rather hear stories —
how so and so
cruised the beach
after the bars
watching those leather daddies
on the hill
spying their prey.

Having been down there once
I thought it pointless
strutting around,
looking disinterested
like I was shell hunting.

The baths are equally predatorial;
lie around, stroll around
in towels everyone wears
make eye contact,
get a massage, a blow-job,
a better view
in the porno room,
from the hot tub,
the steam room.

Sex is hierarchical:

buff boys do it
to buff boys who do it

to pretty boys
who are really glam boys
who do it
to other glam boys
who stay clear of big daddies
who do it to anyone

willing.

One time
these clumsy hands on my stomach
made me think —
how the smallest of intimacies
are smothered, lost
when there's no spirit.

I Want

I want
to celebrate, celebrate men
the way a bee
celebrates pollen,
the way
wind celebrates rain
carries it to my nose,
tips of fingers,
tip of tongue

I want

a ceremony celebrating kinship,
friendship, courtship,
partnership
to be comfortable enough
in my bones
to state the obvious
if need be

I want

duel ceremonies;
one to celebrate
bad hair, bad breath,
bad moods, bad food,
bad jokes, bad days
the other celebrating
baseball caps, Scope,
anti-depressants, take-out,
Cable TV, the unmade bed

I want

to lie in, pick at cherries,
savour the back-rub,
lull my lover
back to dreams, rise
eventually, celebrate

the kiss

coming & going.

Song For Dean

Three years ago
he was the ghost
breathing heat
on winter nights.

Now it's Friday morning
far beyond reason
and I crave his touch
like slivers of glass, soft
unsuspecting needles
beckoning
one perfect drop of crimson
to the surface.

Three years ago
the dreams were of
doves and bare rooms —
the only sound
his mouth thirsting.
Three years ago
the dreams
kept me in bed,
imploring a beginning,
an ending.

Now
I want only shadows,
rain, a lulling memory
drifting back
his voice.

It is Friday morning
far beyond reason
and I sing to myself —

Dean,
if ever there is love
between men
I wish your eyes
endless moons, my hands
the ocean
in which you drown.

3

The Urban Rez

Tough Times On Moccasin Blvd

Battered rez dog look
Sulking down up back again
Zigzag the usual dopers ducking

Behind the hotel dumpster
Divers do it for free
These addicts sit defeated corpses

Crouched on their hunchback bone
Bent and twisted hovering over
A singular dirty rig

Pricks transparent skin holding together
A framework of jelly bones inside
Shooting galleries they sprawl

On a beat up mattress tripping
On their rez dog tongues wagging
And drool and bob their shrunken heads

Up down up down and
Down the street they zigzag
Flock starved like pigeons and

Hover around the needle van
Shrieking obscure dialect and shriek
Their rez dog mumbo-jumbo

Earsplitting as a mausoleum
scattering the shouts of death
Up down and back again

Fix

"What happened to her teeth?" I ask
not that it's any of my business
and put in my two cents worth
as if it counts now
she looks like a premature granny
with her lips curled under
the gums like that, drooling
and making those little sucking sounds

I always know
when she's whacked out on junk —
her eyes get so crazy,
two black marbles floating off
in a hundred different directions
making it hard to figure out
what she sees
who knows —
maybe just the air-borne dust
of her worker's voice
going on about detox
or where to get free meals downtown

She can't eat though
that's the whole problem
her guts won't keep anything down
no wonder
it's the junk eating her insides
worse yet the plague
I hope not
she hasn't got the tell-tale marks
at least from what I can see

only her cough
doesn't seem to clear up

One time I asked her outright
"Are you sick?"
she was too strung out to answer
she was on the nod
mumbling something about an old foster home
she wanted me to help her
to a standing position
her mouth was more caved in
than ever

Holding up her boney frame
I had to wonder
if those twig legs would carry her
to the next block, if she'd be able
to muster up a toothless grin
for her next fix

Day's Work

for C.

Thursday
her body was found
wrapped in plastic
dumped
like rotten garbage
for the media crows
to pick over
and haggle
what the headlines
should read

Friday
the news came
flooding
down the stroll
and into the office
The first word
was Tara's
dazed and bouncing hollow
against the walls

Saturday
the story blazed
hot and spread rumours
she'd been stabbed
beyond recognition
A black 4X4
was spotted
cruising
deep in the city
the cops

were on the look-out
for the tranny sister
who'd seen her
climb in

Monday
her school stuff arrived
and waited
to be opened
That was the ticket
we hoped
off the street

Tuesday
no word except
to say
the body would be released
following the autopsy
Her family said
bury it
where ever we want

Three weeks snail by
we watch the crows
kaw and screech
blast the silence
waiting
a decent rest

tipiskâk / Tonight

Like great *Cheechum*
I scurry about,
a watchful beetle dodging shadows
taking the sage smudge
from room to room,
waving feathers, sprinkling tobacco
in four corners.

Before bed
the dishes get covered,
the crumbs swept away
and I sit quiet
smoking, the hours before light
drifting above my head
like the one
who wasn't called home.

Cheechum: great grandmother

Another Street Kid Just Died

I don't even know his real name or what rez he escaped
from. Somewhere in Alberta I think because of his
accent. He never said much when I was out doing
streetwork. Only yes to condoms & lube. His tricks
just thought he was some exotic Indian rent-a-princess.
But we heard he did a lot for the Two-Spirited people.
He was their tranny-granny keeping them all in check.
He even knew how to give them shit without saying
anything. Now we wonder if he jumped or was pushed
out the hotel window downtown. Last week around
the office I found out he had the plague.

Shaky Ground

The days I'm most expected
to be reliable, giving
are the days
I want to scream, Fuck you
leave me alone,
get a job, a life,
a grip.
Instead
I doddle in late
dreaming poetry,
the next day off
to write it.

Nights
I don't sleep well
pecking at words, cursing
my mush brain
and the worker
I should have called,
the hospital visit
I didn't make,
the meeting
I was supposed to attend.

Then that little bitch
wannabe street mama
says she saw me
blitzed out of my tree
the other night —
how so I say
been on the wagon eight years

and wondering now
why;

the poems of course,
the sacred birthing place
where the steady finger
begins

the head unwinds,
the heart flows
freely

like all these street tongues
wagging.

Cycle (of the black lizard)

It was a priest
who made him act that way
so shy he wouldn't say shit
if his mouth was full of it.
At least that's what his
old lady said
each time her face got smashed
with his drunk fist.
The last time
he just pushed her around
then passed out.
Later, her *kôhkum* said
a lizard crawled inside his mouth
and laid eggs.

It was a black lizard, she said
the kind who eat the insides
feasting slowly
until their young are hatched.
Already his tongue was gone
from so much confessing.
Other boys at the boarding school
never talked out loud
for fear the lizard
would creep into their beds.
At first it just moved around
inside his head
manoeuvring serpentine
like a bad dream.

Then one night
his brain caved in & oozed out
his ears, nose and mouth.

It was his mouth
that caused so much trouble.
In there was rotten teeth
and stink breath
made by that gluttonous lizard.
Morning Mass
he swallowed hard to rid the slime
but nighttime it just returned
and slithered around.

Another boy, only older
had the same trouble.
Recess
they eyed each other's dirty holes
and spit, spit, spit.
Once they got caught
and had to scrub the stairs —
and neither said shit about it.

At school, the teacher
noticed his kids had dull eyes
and never spoke or laughed.
The girl was ten
and developed for her age.
When asked in class to tell an Indian story

she went crimson in her face
and cried.
Every few days
her brother got sent
to the principal's office.
They thought he was just naturally rough,
like all Indians.
What they didn't know
was in her pee-hole, his mouth
a lizard crawled around
leaving eggs
during the Lord's prayer.

---

kôhkum: grandmother

Purple Moon Café

Back booth minding my business
Purple moon under her eye
Mouth puffed so words float

Thick off her tongue
Waft over cracked heads,
Spiral past glazed eyes

No one sees, no one hears
How his fist connected, how
He emptied the black rage

Redecorated her face
To match the surroundings:
The dented hot-plate,

The lumpy bed, the puke-green floors
Where roaches scurried
Beneath the dangling bulb, where

The anger subsided, his hands
Grew heavy on breasts, between thighs
His throat grunting

What a slut she is
To allow even his finger
Inside

The café, minding my business
Purple moon under her eye
Mouth puffed

So words float thick
And the coffee goes down
A curdled, muttering lump

How Many White People Noticed
(and recounted the scene over dinner)

Outside the Dodson
the scene wasn't as disturbing
as seeing a wino
plunge twelve stories or
hearing the fatal crack
of a human skull
upon impact.
Still, by the way she landed
she must have went down
like a ton of bricks.

At first
I thought she was a goner.
Then I saw
her fingers twitch.
"She's had it, eh?" some drunk said,
wobbling down beside her.
"You her old man?" I asked,
moving in
so he couldn't cop a free feel.

A crowd assembled, mostly drunks
from other boozecans
along 100 block.
9-1-1 said turn her on her side,
clear her mouth, tilt her head back,
talk calmly, wait.
Brushing back her hair I saw
she was in her early twenties.
Her face was smooth
and free of bruises —

I could tell
she did't put up with any shit.

Finally the paramedics arrived.
Having checked her vital signs
and finding them satisfactory
they shook her so roughly
she opened up her eyes.
"How much have you had
to drink today?"
"Hey, how much have you had
to drink today?"
"HOW MUCH HAVE YOU HAD
TO DRINK TODAY?"

Her eyes floated over
and discovered me slowly.
"My boy's in care," she slurrred,
grabbing my hand,
"I gotta see my worker."

Across the street
a businessman sat in his car
watching the entire scene.
Only after she was up
and staggering towards Pigeon Park
did he leave, grinning
as smart as
the clatter of china, the clinking
of knives on crystal,
always the knives, I thought
their goddamn knives.

That Squawman Went Free

On the street   it had been leaked
by the looks of her
he'd slapped her around
enough damn times
to make himself feel better
how he couldn't get a real woman —
a whitewoman to hop

Every week his mouth
plastered to her tits
those fat stub fingers
dug in her spoon
craving a shrivelled dick cure
he even made her suck
the useless gut   and blamed her

The money went up her nose or
in her arms — when the veins collapsed
she used her legs
her skid sister said
sometimes he had the decency
to wait until the bruises healed
before he picked her up again

Last month her body was discovered
by the railroad tracks — they figured
another Native suicide / overdose
but there was some talk
about a bad date
someone reported his licence plate number —
all we heard was
    Welfare flew her home

No Fuss

for the lost sisters

Tromping through our skid row rez
All their hoopla over one whitewoman spreads
Hot across my red red face
Even at Oka there wasn't this much fuss
Maybe our women don't have that all-American
Blond bombshell taxpayer look that's required
To get attention — or action depending on what type you are

Why shout or beat my deerhide drum
I don't need the cops busting me for spray painting
Their protest with my graffiti lips
When I want justice I just shoot off my mouth on paper
That way I don't make easy target practice
Unless of course I get too truthful at a reading
Then it might be curtains for me

Mouthing off the way I am right now
But I always seize the chance
Chance is I could go on til I'm blue in the face
But what difference would it make
Their fuss isn't demanding the cops
Get off their extended Indian donut break
They want the bastard strung up for not snuffing a squaw

Even her dad got in good with the media
Bragged how he suffered the tortuous interviews
My daughter was so beautiful, he said,
It's beyond words, I need a good producer
When it finally comes to our turn
I'm fair enough to know
I'll be the first to join those sisters in the ghost chant

Leftovers

Brown bags on a beach budget
Work hard for a meal
White bags are darn choosy
What snack they take home
Summer they're all beach bums lounging
Whose tan disappears come winter
City bears are fat & lie around snoring
No hotdogs worth begging
Wild ones know who's a stupid camper
They take first without asking
Shoplifters do it at the Safeway
Ducking a criminal record
Not a tranquilizer dart
Soup lines & food banks are free
But not ethnic
Traditional Indians stay home
For the rounddance
Cakes & bannock
Go in a handy ice cream pail
For good munching on later

Street Rite

we got the right to speak /
slurred unrefined English
if we want to /
yell in the back alley
or talk tough to a pawn broker /
okay / when I say I want 50
that doesn't mean 20

we got the right to take over the city /
spray paint it
with our very own rez lingo / if we want
take out around the clock
that's up to us /
when I want sushi
that means now not later

we got the right to dance drunk
on cheap / okay / if we want to
run up a tab / give our IOU /
who says we can't /
when I'm low on *sônîyâs*
I don't want the usual whiney ho-hum

we got the right to eye 'em
'n' tease 'em
those desperate wannabes / if we want to
make our commando charge
ALL WAGONS WEST or
ALL WAGONS BACK TO OUR PLACE / why not /
when I say *wâk-wâh*
that's really cuddle up *nîcimos*
and do it *sîmak*

we got the right to chi-chi cuisine
not these dumpster left-overs /
if we want
good service or a piano concerto
to help digest on a limited budget /
why kiss up their asses /
when I want class
that's not Hank Williams
chomping on a half-eaten hotdog

we got the right to demand
a full scale city investigation /
if we want / police accountability
or racial equality / that's now /
when I want accurate representation
I don't want just any
legal aid Rambo / I want
a smooth Armani lawyer / so does
that big hyena skinhead
looking down on me

---

sônîyâs: money
wâk-wâh: equivalent to "Oh, my goodness"
nîcimos: sweetheart or lover
sîmak: right now or right away

Piss 'n' Groan

When the sun comes out
the streets smell like piss
down here
it doesn't matter what side
of the skids
you're on
you could be better than me
I really don't give a damn
if you think so
why not just say so
I won't crumble
because you got a swollen-up head

That lump could be
from a wagon burner like me
who wouldn't play the dirty Indian
just off the rez role
because you got an inferiority complex
being one of the few
under-classy winos
who can't afford to be
a white alcoholic   unlike me
I got so much lower-class
I far surpass
their usual upper-class groan

How they got to pay taxes
and we don't
as if we said 500 years ago
put that in the treaty
while you're at it

roll out that whiskey keg
and don't forget to include
an educational clause
if we're going to be force-fed
your glamorous take-over history
why not get paid to act
the conquered part   the part where we say
hey, *môniyâs* I want my cheque
gimme my cheque right now
you owe me
for this left-over land
we never sold, gave up, handed over

Don't tell me
we got no rights here
just because you got the Legislation
to steal and expropriate
without our consent
that doesn't mean
there was no law here
before you stuck your big toe
across the line   tap danced all over
the continent like it was yours
to begin with
why all this pissing and groaning
whether we got the inherent right
to stop you from dumping
your pesticides or polluting the planet

Who needs all that colonial crap anyway
saying I'm just another

loud mouth Indian
rattling off anti-white propaganda
is justification that any cohesive
future together is pissed away already
because you don't want to hear
all my pissing 'n' groaning
even if I suggested
we piss 'n' groan collectively
that still wouldn't heal
the damage done
maybe even now
I've groaned more harm than good
but who gives a damn
my groaning job is throwing it all back
to look at
whoever wants to get pissy
go right ahead
I'm not gonna cry about it

---

môniyâs: non-native person

Warrior Mask

This face
wasn't always
a concrete mask
littered in neon
to be spit, frowned
or pissed on.

In puberty
my *Âyahkwêw* eyes
followed strangers
and saw the black junk
squishing
around inside.

The face
came one night
when a grandfather
worked his medicine
in a dream.

"*Sâwanohk*," he said
softly, mixing pollen and spit
he covered the right side
completely and
gave me summer songs
to sing.

A black line divided.

"*Pahkisimotâhk*," he continued
grinding charcoal, spitting

and mixing and
marked four black dots
on the left.

"*Â,*" he clapped,
"your path to the spirits."
"*nikamow,*" *itêw,* "*nikamow.*"

Âyahkwêw: loosely translated as a person who has both male and female
    spirits; also known as Two-Spirited
Sâwanohk: south
Pahkisimotâhk: west
Â: exlaimation or acknowledgement
"*nikamow,*" *itêw,* "*nikamow*": "Sing," he said, "sing."

The Poet Leaves A Parting Thought

hâw, ni-nêhiyawêyân and
their English tags behind my every word
word is my rez city lingo
is good enough to get
a bonafide hmm from the white audience
maybe even a raised eyebrow
if I really wow 'em 'n' schmooze 'em
with my dangling modifier talk
in my own Indigenous way
I can be pretty preverbed
when I want

appropriate recognition
I get the usual inconclusive oh
although my buffalo robe talk
can be darn sexy
when I flavour it up with some Cree spice
why waste my breath
on Columbus hot talk
I just end up making him into
a Don Juan hero
as if his slaver descendants
deserve that fame

but it could happen
if I don't give my tongue
a native language mammogram
check it regularly
for English lumps and bumps
I run the chance of becoming
totally anglicized

I wouldn't understand if an elder said
âtayohikî, boy
I'd have to go back to school
for proper instruction

then I'd be just another wannabe book-talker
not an Indigenous oral talker like I am
but a multicultural professor
talker / bragger
bragging how I know up-shot Indians
but what's there to brag about bragging
I don't make 70,000 a year
doing anthropological digs in Peru
more like AIDS studies
because I see these corpses daily
dragging themselves around the city

looking for food or shelter
they just keep popping up
new off the rez
need a place to stay
nowhere to go except Catholic Charities
a transition house
if you're really black 'n' blue
maybe detox
if you've been on an extended bender
I make the appropriate referral
go home scream and write

create dark talk
for white talkers to talk about

I might not be the best
Indigenous poet
but hey, my English is lousy enough
to be honest

---

hâw, ni-nêhiyawêyân: now, I speak Cree
âtayohikî: to tell a legend or myth

preverbed: in between a verb and perverted

Cree Translations

Â: exlaimation or acknowledgement

âcimowina: stories

ahcâhk: spirit

âskaw kâ-tipiskâk: sometimes at night

âtayohikî: to tell a legend or myth

Âyahkwêw: loosely translated as a person who has both male and female spirits; also known as Two-Spirited

ayamihâwina: rituals

cheechum: great grandmother

êkospî ê-miyoskamik: that spring

êkospî ê-pipohk: that winter

êkospî kâ-kî-pîkiskwêt: when he spoke

êkospî kâ-nîpihk: that summer

êkospî kâ-tipiskâk: that night

êkwa êkosi, nikîwêhtatânân ôhi mistatimwak: And so, we brought these horses home

êkwa êkosi kîtohta: and so, listen

Hai-Hai Nitotemak: Thanks To My Relations

hâw, ni-nêhiyawêyân: now, I speak Cree

hâw-nikiskisin: now, I remember

iyee: exclamation of disgust or disdain

iyiniwak: people

kâ-miyoskamik: springtime

kaskitêw-maskwa / nimâmâ: my black bear / mother

katipâmsôchik: The People Who Own Themselves

kâya kakwêchihkêmaw: don't ask

kîmôc: sneaky or sly

kinêpik: snake

Kisê-manitow: The Creator or Great Mystery

kîwetinohk: the north

kôhkum: grandmother

la-pataka: potatoes

mâkêsis: fox

mâmitonêyihchikâna: memories

mâsawêwin: sexual
maskêkiyiniwak: doctors
Mistatim-awâsis: Horse-child
môniyâs: non-native person
mosôm: grandfather
nâpêwak: men
nehiyaw: Indian
ni-âcimon: autobiography or My Story
nîcimos: sweetheart or lover
"nikamow," itêw, "nikamow": "Sing," he said, "sing."
nîsto-maskwak: Three Bears
nitim: sister-in-law
nôhkom: grandmother
nôhkomâk: grandmothers
ochichisa: her hands
Pahkisimotâhk: west
pahkwêsikan: bannock
Paskowi-pîsim: July or the Moulting Moon
pekîwe: come home
pîkiskwewina: words
pîpîsis: baby
Piyesîwak-iskwêw: Thunder-woman
Sâwanohk: south
sîmak: right now or right away
sîpihko-nâpêsis: Blue Boy (as in the painting)
skônak: female dog; also, a sexually promiscuous person
sônîyâs: money
sôskwac itôta: just do it
tahto kîsikâw: every day
tipiskâk: tonight
wâk-wâh: Oh my goodness
Wîhtikôw: cannibal or Ice Being
Wîsahkecâhk: First Man or Cree Trickster
wiyâs: meat